FANTASY FILMS

Matt Anniss

Badger Publishing Limited
Oldmeadow Road,
Hardwick Industrial Estate,
King's Lynn PE30 4JJ
Telephone: 01438 791 037

www.badgerlearning.co.uk

2 4 6 8 10 9 7 5 3 1

Fantastic Films ISBN 978-1-78464-375-1

Publisher: Susan Ross
Project editor: Paul Rockett
Senior editor: Danny Pearson
Editorial coordinator: Claire Morgan
Designer: Jason Billin / BDS Publishing Ltd

Picture credits: AF archive/Alamy: 16, 22; Everett Collection/Shutterstock.com: 1,10, 27;
famouspeople/Alamy: 9; Felix Lipov/Shutterstock.com: 12; GOLFX/Shutterstock.com: cover, 29;
Chris Harvey/Shutterstock.com 4, 15; Jaguar PS/Shutterstock.com: 28; Luca Marella/Dreamstime.
com: 14; MJTH/Shutterstock.com: 5; Moviestore collection Ltd/Alamy: 13, 30; Photos 12/Alamy:
21, 24; Pictorial Press Ltd/Alamy: 6, 11, 18; Radiokafka/Shutterstock.com: 25; Wikimedia
Commons: 20; World History Archive/Alamy: 26.

Attempts to contact all copyright holders have been made. If any omitted would care to
contact Badger Learning, we will be happy to make appropriate arrangements.

Contents

Vocabulary

Do you know these words? Look them up in a dictionary and then see how they are used in the book.

amassed	inspire
exploits	monstrous
franchises	quest
futuristic	transferred

CHAPTER 1

MAGNIFICENT MYSTERIES

Have you ever read a book and thought 'This would make a great film'?

If so, you're not alone. Every year, many filmmakers try to make their favourite books into movies.

Films based on books are known as 'adaptations'. This is because the filmmakers have 'adapted' an existing story and turned it into a movie. As we'll prove, great books often make fantastic films!

★★ FACT! ★★

Trilby and Little Billee, made in 1896, may well be cinema's first book adaptation. The silent, black-and-white movie is based on a scene from George Du Maurier's book Trilby.

5

★ PAPER TOWNS ★

Actors Cara Delevigne and Nat Wolff in the film of Paper Towns.

It can take years for a book to be turned into a film. The mystery novel *Paper Towns*, a story about a teenager's quest to find his missing friend, hit bookstores in 2008. The film version opened in cinemas seven years later.

Although John Green wrote the book, he didn't write the film version. Instead, a team of specialist 'screenwriters' adapted his story for the big screen.

Paper Towns wasn't the first novel by John Green to make it to the big screen. His 2012 story about two teenagers with cancer, *The Fault in Our Stars*, was turned into a movie in 2014.

The book is one of the best selling novels for young adults of all time. The movie was even more successful, racking up a whopping £196 million in ticket sales.

★★ FACT! ★★

The books of English writer Charles Dickens have proved hugely popular with filmmakers. According to the Internet Movie Database, his novels have inspired over 340 films and TV shows!

The makers of the 2011 movie *Hugo* had an easier job than John Green's screenwriters. That's because the movie is based on Brian Selznick's book, *The Invention of Hugo Cabret*, which features lots of pictures as well as words.

Selznick's drawings inspired many of the most memorable scenes in the film adaptation.

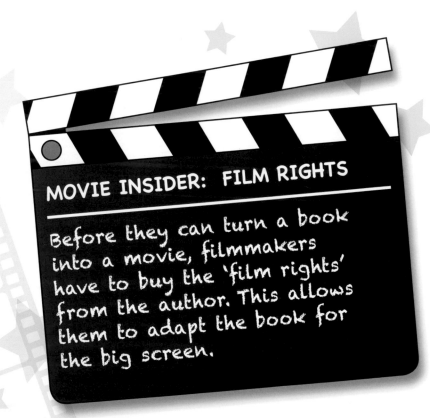

MOVIE INSIDER: FILM RIGHTS

Before they can turn a book into a movie, filmmakers have to buy the 'film rights' from the author. This allows them to adapt the book for the big screen.

THE DAILY NEWS

REAL LIFE MYSTERY

The 2014 Oscar-winning film *The Imitation Game* was based on the real life story of one man's quest to solve the biggest mystery of the Second World War.

It was loosely based on Andrew Hodges' book *The Enigma*, which detailed the life of brilliant British mathematician Alan Turing. During the war, Turing invented a machine that helped the Allies to crack the Nazi's top-secret coded messages.

Alan Turing

Some of the greatest movie adaptations are those based on adventure stories – fast-paced novels packed full of exciting events.

Few adventure stories are quite as thrilling as the magical exploits of the young wizards featured in J.K. Rowling's *Harry Potter* novels. To date, over 450 million *Harry Potter* books have been sold.

Eight films were made of the series' seven books. They were wildly successful, earning the filmmakers an astonishing £5 billion in ticket sales!

The Harry Potter *films made stars of its three lead actors Rupert Grint, Daniel Radcliffe and Emma Watson (pictured below).*

Film still from the movie The Maze Runner.

Author James Dashner loves films. He says that before he wrote *The Maze Runner* in 2009, he imagined the story as an action-packed movie.

Children and young adults who've read the book often say that it is as quick, eventful and exciting as a brilliant film. It was therefore not much of a surprise when it was turned into a movie in 2014.

★★ FACT! ★★

2012's *Life of Pi*, based on the novel of the same name by Yann Martel, made an astonishing £401 million in cinema ticket sales.

It would have been hard to make a film version of J.R.R. Tolkien's classic fantasy novel, *The Hobbit*, when it was written in 1937.

The book was finally turned into three films between 2012 and 2014. Director Peter Jackson used 21st century special effects to bring Tolkien's imaginary worlds and fantastical characters to life.

MOVIE INSIDER: BIG BUDGETS

Each of the three *Hobbit* films cost £163 million to make. Even by Hollywood standards, that's expensive!

Walt Disney's 1967 cartoon film *The Jungle Book* is still hugely popular. The 2016 and 2017 re-makes, both featuring a mixture of actors and animated animals, may yet be even more popular.

Did you know that the films are based on stories written by Rudyard Kipling over 120 years ago? Kipling's *The Jungle Book*, charting the adventures of an orphan brought up by animals, was first published in 1894.

★★ FACT! ★★

The 1984 film *The NeverEnding Story*, based on a novel by Michael Ende, is now considered by many to be a classic. Ende famously hated it and demanded his name was removed from the credits!

Versions of the Bible, the book on which several religions are based, have existed for thousands of years.

It's perhaps unsurprising that the amazing stories contained in the Bible have inspired many films over the years, including:

★ *Noah* (2014)
★ *Exodus: Gods & Kings* (2014)
★ *Son of God* (2014)
★ *The Ten Commandments* (2007)

The story of Noah's Ark has been an inspiration for paintings, drawings, musicals as well as movies.

CHAPTER 3

SERIOUS SCIENCE FICTION

Do you enjoy reading books and watching films that have storylines built around aliens, the end of the world or futuristic technology?

If the answer is 'yes', you could be a fan of science fiction. Sci-fi novels first became popular nearly 100 years ago, and film adaptations have been appearing ever since.

Science fiction fans dressed up as their favourite characters for a sci-fi film convention.

Classic sci-fi novels that have been made into movies include:

★ *Frankenstein* by Mary Shelley
★ *The War of the Worlds* by H. G. Wells
★ *Journey to the Centre of the Earth* by Jules Verne

Film still from the movie Rise of the Planet of the Apes.

The best sci-fi novels often inspire a large number of film adaptations. Pierre Boule's 1963 novel *Planet of the Apes* is a great example. The story was first turned into a movie in 1968.

The movie was re-made in 2001, and Boule's book continues to inspire filmmakers. *Rise of the Planet of the Apes* appeared in 2011, with *Dawn of the Planet of the Apes* following three years later.

Michael Crichton's 1990 novel about a theme park full of dinosaurs, *Jurassic Park*, sold nine million copies in the three years following its publication.

More books and three film adaptations soon followed. A fourth movie, *Jurassic World*, was released in 2015.

MOVIE INSIDER: FRANCHISES

Planet of the Apes and *Jurassic Park* are examples of 'movie franchises'. This is what film experts call a series of films featuring the same characters, setting or theme.

Another successful sci-fi franchise is *The Hunger Games*. It started out as a wildly successful series of novels by author Suzanne Collins. To date, over 50 million copies of the three books have been sold.

Collins' story, featuring a dark, futuristic world of deadly game shows and gangs of teenagers, was made into four films between 2012 and 2015.

★★ FACT! ★★

Thanks to both the books and film versions of *The Hunger Games*, Suzanne Collins has amassed an estimated personal fortune of over £37 million.

Veronica Roth was just 22 years old when she wrote *Divergent*, the first of three novels in the series.

The novels explore similar ideas to *The Hunger Games*. Just like that series, Roth's books have been turned into four films. The first hit cinemas in March 2014, with the remainder being released over the following three years.

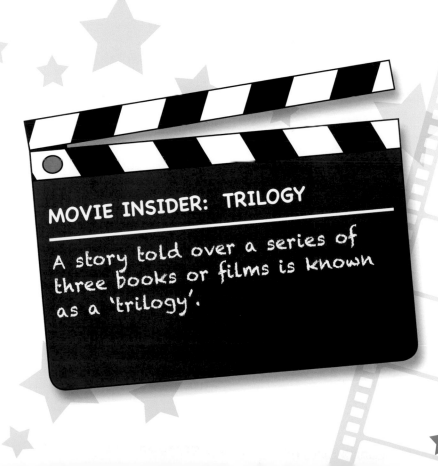

MOVIE INSIDER: TRILOGY

A story told over a series of three books or films is known as a 'trilogy'.

An illustrated scene from the fairy tale Cinderella.

Filmmakers can adapt all types of stories, old or new. Few stories are older than fairy tales. According to historians, parents have been telling their children fairy tales for hundreds and even thousands of years.

These stories, some of which have been turned into brilliant books by writers such as Hans Christian Andersen and the Brothers Grimm, continue to inspire today's moviemakers.

Actor Angelina Jolie in the title role of Maleficent.

You might have seen the movie *Maleficent*, Disney's 2014 version of the *Sleeping Beauty* fairy tale.

The story became popular in the 19th century, when it was included in *Children's and Household Tales* by the Brothers Grimm. Historians have traced the story back much further and now think it was first written in France around 1340!

Like *Sleeping Beauty*, the *Beauty and the Beast* fairy tale first appeared in a French book. The popular story, about a young woman falling in love with a monster, was written in 1740.

The story has inspired a number of films, most notably Disney's 1991 cartoon version. The fairy tale reappeared in cinemas in 2011 as *Beastly*.

Beastly transferred the story to modern-day New York, and featured a teenager being turned into a horrible monster in order to find true love.

A new film version of *Beauty and the Beast*, starring *Harry Potter* actress Emma Watson, is due to hit cinemas in 2017.

MOVIE INSIDER: FREE STORIES

Filmmakers like centuries-old fairy tales, because they don't have to pay a 'rights fee'. Stories as old as these can be re-told in film form completely free of charge.

SNOW WHITE AND THE HUNTSMAN

Actors Kristen Stewart and Chris Hemsworth in the title roles from Snow White and the Huntsman.

Because fairy tales are so well known, filmmakers sometimes give the stories a new twist in order to surprise audiences. This is what the makers of *Snow White and the Huntsman* did in 2012.

In the original Brothers Grimm fairy tale, Snow White is a young woman who needs protecting from an evil queen. In the 2012 film she joins forces with a huntsman to track down and fight the queen.

CHAPTER 5

SUPERHEROES AND VICIOUS VILLAINS

According to industry statistics, over 82 million comic books were sold in 2014. That's a lot of potential fans for superhero movies!

Some of the most popular films of our times aren't based on traditional books, but rather characters from comics.

Ever since the first Superman comic appeared in 1938, filmmakers have been putting superheroes on the big screen. The first superhero to hit the big screen was Captain Marvel, way back in 1941!

Since then, classic comic book characters, such as Spider-Man, Batman and Superman, have appeared in countless films.

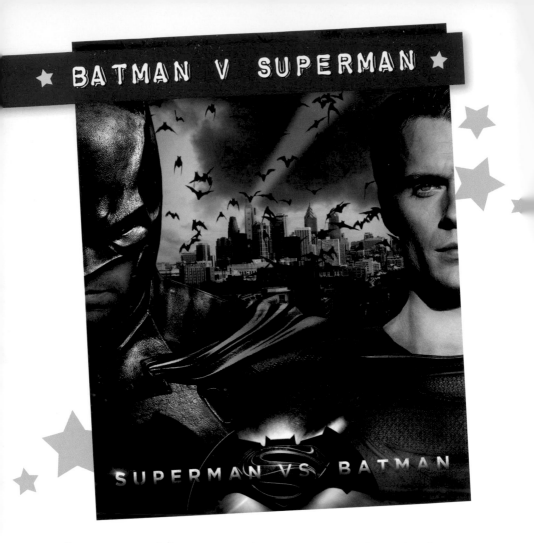

SUPERMAN VS BATMAN

Batman and Superman have appeared on the big screen many times, but only once together. 2016's *Batman v Superman: Dawn of Justice* sees DC Comics' most famous superheroes do battle.

While *Batman v Superman: Dawn of Justice* isn't based on a particular comic book, the two superheroes have faced each other in print before. Their battle forms part of the storyline to Frank Miller's 1986 comic series, *The Dark Knight Returns*.

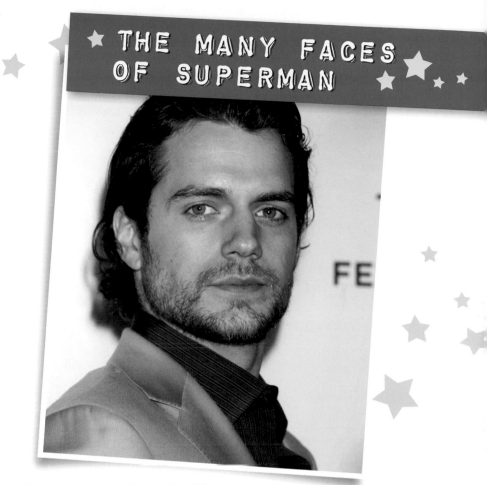

Superman actor Henry Cavill

The first actor to play Superman on the big screen was Kirk Alyn in 1948. Since then, the following actors have all portrayed the 'Man of Steel':

★ George Reeves (*Superman and the Mole Men*, 1951)

★ Christopher Reeve (*Superman, Superman II, Superman III, Superman IV: The Quest For Peace*, 1978–87)

★ Brandon Routh (*Superman Returns*, 2006)

★ Henry Cavill (*Man of Steel, Batman v Superman*, 2013–16)

Stan Lee is one of the most successful comic book writers of all time. Many of his heroes and villains have made it onto the big screen.

The most famous is Spider-Man, whose story has been told on screen many times. There was a trilogy of films about the web-slinging crime fighter in the 2000s, and two more under *The Amazing Spider-Man* title between 2012 and 2014. The story is being given another 're-boot' with a new Spider-Man film due out in 2017.

Andrew Garfield played the lead character in The Amazing Spider-Man *films.*

In 1963, Stan Lee and cartoonist Jack Kirby created a comic book series about an ever-changing team of superheroes known as the Avengers. It featured classic characters such as Iron Man, The Hulk, Thor, Captain America and, occasionally, Spider-Man.

It took until 2012 for an Avengers film to appear in cinemas. It was an enormous box office hit, earning the filmmakers over a billion US dollars! A follow-up, *Avengers: Age of Ultron* was released in 2015.

Since 2008, the character of Iron Man has appeared in his own successful film franchise.

GUARDIANS OF THE GALAXY

The futuristic superheroes of *Guardians of the Galaxy* first appeared in a comic way back in 1969. In 2008, Marvel Comics decided to re-start the series featuring a whole set of new characters.

It was this modern re-make, rather than the original, which inspired the 2014 *Guardians of the Galaxy* movie. The film famously contains one major character from the 1969 version, Yondu.

How many actors have played Superman in films? *(page 27)*

★ ★ ★ ★ ★ ★

How many copies of *The Hunger Games* books have been sold to date? *(page 18)*

★ ★ ★ ★ ★ ★

How much did each of *The Hobbit* films cost to make? *(page 12)*

★ ★ ★ ★ ★ ★

What was the name of the book that inspired the film *Hugo*? *(page 8)*

★ ★ ★ ★ ★ ★

In what year was Pierre Boule's novel *The Planet of The Apes* first published? *(page 16)*

★ ★ ★ ★ ★ ★

What is a 'trilogy'? *(page 19)*

★ ★ ★ ★ ★ ★

★ INDEX ★